CUT IT, SEW IT, STOW IT™

Annie's®

Organizing in Style

The world is full of plastic containers, and it seems a shame to let them dominate our organizing lives with their bland exteriors when there are so many more beautiful colors, textures and shapes to be achieved with fabric.

As you work through this book, you'll find an organizer that's suitable for nearly every room in your home. Along with the project, there is a tip for organizing that space, so as you add new organizers to the room, you can take the clutter out.

Each project also provides an opportunity to learn a new skill or incorporate a technique you may not have tried. Do zippers send shivers down your spine? You'll find two fearless techniques in the Stowaway Pillow Cover and Wardrobe Accessory Hanger projects. Does your machine have decorative stitches you've never tried? Give them a workout on the Closet Hanging Pockets or Craft Room Hanging Buckets.

*Entryway Mail & Key Trays, **page 13***

These projects also make great containers for gifts; consider the Kitchen Bag Hamper as a unique housewarming gift. Include some towels, hot pads and serving utensils and you will have created a wonderful presentation in a reusable box.

I hope you love making these projects as much as I enjoyed designing them for you!

Meet the Designer

Ebony Love, award-winning quilter and owner of LoveBug Studios, is recognized as one of the leading experts in fabric die-cutting techniques. She regularly produces free videos featuring tips and techniques for die cutting and quilting. Although Ebony is more recognizable these days as a quilting personality, her love of sewing started at an early age when she made costumes and evening gowns for herself and others.

Born in Denver, Colo., Ebony has lived all over the United States but now calls the Midwest home. Ebony earned a bachelor of science in industrial engineering from Columbia University and a master of science in engineering from Purdue University.

Sewing and quilting have turned out to be the perfect medium to exercise her love of engineering and math!

She is the author of several quilting books, including *The Big Little Book of Fabric Die Cutting Tips*, and the *Adventures in Fabric Die Cutting* series. Ebony is a recurring guest on *Quilty* (available on QNNtv.com) and has had her quilts, articles and quilting featured in several publications.

Previous Publications
The Big Little Book of Fabric Die Cutting Tips, November 2012, 978-1-938889-00-4
Notes and Doodles: A Die Cutting Sketchbook, January 2013, 978-1-938889-01-1
Adventures in Fabric Die Cutting: The Pyramid Cutting Caper, Summer 2013, 978-1-938889-03-5

Table of Contents

Playroom Toy Baskets, page 46

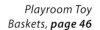

Mudroom Hanging Pockets Organizer, page 7

Plastic Bag Hamper, page 24

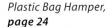

Bedside Saddlebag, page 37

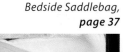

Some techniques may be familiar to you, and others may be new. Regardless, all the techniques you'll need to complete the projects are detailed in this section.

Basic Sewing Techniques

Make It Simple, Make It Fancy

All of the projects in this book offer a simple version and an embellished version. You can choose whether you want to incorporate that embellishing technique or not. The instructions will indicate where in the process you will need to make a decision about embellishing the project with the recommended technique and where to continue the construction process when the embellishing has been completed.

Pay attention to fabric requirements and cutting instructions. These will specifically state additional materials needed or special cutting instructions if they are different between simple and fancy versions.

Basting

Basting is used to temporarily secure pieces to each other until they can be permanently fixed through other construction methods. Spray basting is useful for securing large pieces of fabric to a stabilizer or other surface. Machine basting can hold layers when spray basting might be impractical.

Machine Basting

Lengthen your stitch length to the longest stitch your machine allows. Use a narrow zipper foot or other edge-stitching foot to stitch near the edge through all layers. The basting is typically done within the seam allowance.

Spray Basting

Always follow the manufacturer's instructions to cover one surface (usually the interfacing) with the adhesive spray. Apply the wrong side of fabric to the adhesive surface, smoothing as you go. Be careful not to leave bubbles, wrinkles or folds in the fabric. The spray should allow you to reposition the fabric for a few minutes after application, before requiring another application.

Reinforcing Seams

Reinforcing stitches are used to secure areas of high stress or places where seam allowances are trimmed to reduce bulk. This extra stitching helps to ensure the projects can stand up to wear and tear over time.

Backstitching

Backstitching is achieved by stitching forward, reversing for approximately 1 inch, and then stitching forward again on top of the same seam line.

Echo Stitch

With an echo stitch, you are essentially re-stitching the same seam on top of the seam you just stitched or one thread width away, just inside the seam allowance.

Bar Tacks

This is a zigzag stitch that is stitched back and forth in the same spot. If your machine has decorative stitches, it likely has a built-in bar tack for this purpose. If it does not, set your machine to a zigzag stitch, zero stitch length, using a width that is appropriate for the project. Stitch 6–8 times to secure.

Reducing Bulk

Using many layers of fabric, stabilizer or interfacing can create bulk in areas where it isn't needed or helpful. It is necessary to reduce bulk in these areas to create crisper corners or to make a piece lay flat.

The following trimming techniques can be used in place of clipping seams on curves, especially since the removal of fabric in these areas often helps a curve lay smoothly.

Grading

To grade a seam allowance, the seam allowances are cut different widths to allow them to nest together reducing bulk and laying flat. Trim the seam allowances near the area of the curve or corner only, but leave them intact elsewhere by angling your cut away from the seam line. The seam allowance that will be closest to the project when pressed is trimmed to ⅛ inch wide. The seam allowance on top is trimmed to ¼ inch wide.

Trimming

Trimming the seam allowance is done around the entire seam. After the piece is stitched, cut the seam allowance to approximately ⅛ inch wide.

Topstitching

Topstitching adds detail to a project and can give it a professional-looking finish when done correctly. Topstitching is not a game of speed. To do it well, go slower than you would normally stitch and gently guide your project under the needle. Use the edge of the presser foot as a guide for stitch placement and lengthen your stitch to one that is slightly longer than your normal stitch length. See the Thread section for suggestions on thread weights for topstitching.

Straight-Stitch Topstitching

Use an edging or narrow zipper foot to stitch close to the edge of a finished seam. The narrow zipper foot usually has two sides so you can position the project to the left or right of the needle based on which is easier to stitch.

Decorative-Stitch Topstitching

If you are topstitching with a decorative stitch, use an open-toe presser foot that can accommodate the width of the stitch so you don't break a needle.

Fabric

Don't be afraid to experiment with different fabrics. As a quilter, I gravitate toward quilting-weight 100 percent cotton fabrics, but these projects also lend themselves to other great choices such as linen, microsuede, denim and corduroy. Suggested fabrics are provided with each project, along with the proper interfacings and stabilizers to provide the right support for the suggested fabric.

A Special Note About Denim

Denim is referred to by how much a yard of denim weighs. It is sold in weights of 5–20 ounces. The heavier the denim, the less flexible it is. Keep that in mind when purchasing. As a guideline, jeans are usually made from medium-weight denim (12–14 ounces).

Fabric Width

Throughout the book, all fabrics are assumed to have at least 42 inches of usable width, unless otherwise noted. This width excludes the fabric selvages which should be trimmed off the fabric before cutting. Selvages are woven tighter and do not shrink or stitch like the rest of the yardage.

If you are the type to save your selvages for other projects, make sure you will have what you need before you cut them off the yardage. Not all fabrics are the same width!

Clear Vinyl

Clear vinyl is either sold in precut packages or off the bolt. Do not purchase the fusible kind or you'll get a nasty surprise when you apply vinyl pockets to your projects!

Twenty-gauge or 0.2mm vinyl is the perfect weight for the projects included in this book. It is flexible, easy to sew through, and durable.

Interfacing & Stabilizers

There are so many choices on the market that it can make your head spin! I tried to make it easy for you by choosing a small assortment of products that work well alone and in combination in all of the projects. I use these products so often in my work that I buy them by the bolt, rather than by the yard, whenever possible. You can find specific products listed in the back of the book.

Foam Stabilizer

This stabilizer uses foam that is less than ¼ inch thick and sandwiched between knit fabrics. This comes in a sew-in and fusible version, and gives a wonderful structure and support to many of the organizers in this book.

Fusible Fleece

Fusible fleece is used in place of foam stabilizer in places where extra thickness is not necessary or would add too much bulk to the project.

Heavy-Weight Interfacing

This interfacing adds body and strength without being too rigid. Like foam stabilizer, it comes in sew-in and fusible types. I prefer to use a fusible version, since many times I'm cutting down pieces after they are interfaced, which defeats the purpose of machine basting.

Fusible Grid

This lightweight nonwoven interfacing has an accurate 1-inch grid printed on one side and is fusible on the other. It is lightweight enough that it doesn't impact the drape of most medium-weight fabrics.

Texturizing Fabric

When steam is applied to this product, it will shrink approximately 30 percent. When stitched to an exterior fabric, it creates a fabulous texture around the stitching with the exterior fabric. Because the shrinkage rate is predictable and permanent, you can easily determine the size of exterior fabric you need to cut. It's important not to apply heat or steam before applying the texturizing fabric.

Thread
Threads come in different weights and materials. With the superior technology these days, it's no longer a requirement to use only cotton thread on cotton fabric.

Sewing & Topstitching
I am partial to one particular thread for my sewing, and that's a 50-weight, 100 percent cotton thread. This allows me to have the accuracy I need for the smallest seam allowance I use, and it can stand up to the high heat of my iron. I will occasionally switch to a 40-weight for topstitching when I want the stitching to show more. Use colors that match your project.

Embellishing
Pearl cotton and embroidery floss are the two threads I use most for hand embroidery, couching or other handwork. Embroidery floss typically comes in 6-strand skeins, and usually, the strands are divided before beginning any embroidery. Pearl cotton, on the other hand, is not meant to be divided, so it comes in different weights. Remember, the higher the number, the thinner the thread. I usually work with #5 or #8, but #10 and #12 are also common for more intricate work.

Invisible Work
Monofilament thread is made with either nylon or polyester. It is measured by either the Tex weight, or in millimeters. The larger the Tex number (or number of millimeters), the thicker and stronger the thread.

Nylon monofilament is a little easier to find than polyester in the .005mm size that is recommended in this book. Nylon has a bad reputation for becoming yellow and brittle over time and melting under the heat of an iron. If you're making outdoor furniture, polyester is better in the long run, but for everything else, nylon is probably fine.

Basic Sewing Tools & Supplies
There are several items that every sewer needs in their sewing box. I'm sure you have most of them. Here is a list of the basic items required to construct the projects in this book:

Equipment
- Sewing machine in good working order
- Assorted machine needles in sizes 80/12, 90/14, 100/16 and 110/18
- Variety of threads
- ¼-inch seam presser foot
- Stitch-in-the-ditch foot
- Narrow zipper foot (or edge-stitching foot)
- Pintuck foot (optional)
- Hand-sewing needles with thimble
- Seam ripper

Measuring & Cutting
- Tape measure
- Rotary cutter with replacement blades
- Rotary-cutting mat
- Straightedge/ruler with measurement markings in at least ⅛-inch increments and degree lines (45, 60, 90 degrees)
- Sewing shears
- Small embroidery scissors
- Paper scissors (for cutting templates)

Marking & Pinning
- Removable marking pens for fabric
- Chalk pencil (wax- and clay-free)
- Clear or gridded template plastic (for tracing patterns and making templates)
- 1-inch-wide painter's tape
- Glass-head pins
- Flat-head pins
- Pincushion

Fabric Adhesives
- Seam sealant
- Basting spray
- Glue stick for fabric

Pressing Tools
- Ironing board
- Iron with steam and dry settings
- Press cloths
- Seam roll for pressing narrow seams (optional)
- 1 part vinegar to 9 parts water pressing solution (for setting pleats or removing stubborn creases)
- Point turner ■

I live in a pretty cold climate near Lake Michigan, and over the years, I've collected a wide variety of hats, gloves, scarves and other winter gear that, until recently, resided together in a bin on the floor of my hall closet. It always takes a bit of hunting through the bin to come up with a matching pair of gloves! This closet pocket is a great way to organize lots of things in a relatively small space, and now I have no problem locating my favorite pair of mittens.

You can use these six pockets in many different ways and in many different rooms. One friend suggested organizing rolls of embroidery stabilizer in her sewing room; another friend thought of using it to store her collection of handbags. I'm sure you can think of the perfect place to hang this set of pockets in your house!

Mudroom Hanging Pockets Organizer

ORGANIZING TIP

At the end of each season, take note of items that are damaged, worn, missing or otherwise need replacing. (Think: sandals, sunglasses, gloves, umbrellas, galoshes, etc.) Now go shopping! You're likely to get better prices on items at the end of the season than at the beginning. If you have a growing family, be sure to buy things a couple of sizes larger than currently needed so they will fit the following year.

Finished Size
Hanging Pockets Organizer: 18 x 36 inches

Materials
- 44/45-inch-wide woven fabrics:
    2¾ yards cotton solid
    3¼ yards cotton print
- 1⅛ yards 45-inch-wide heavy-weight fusible interfacing
- 20 inches ⅜-inch-wide ribbon
- 6 (20mm) buttons
- Heavy-duty plastic or metal hanger
- Fabric-glue stick
- Basic sewing supplies and equipment

Cutting

Refer to Cutting Layouts provided on pattern insert for specific cutting instructions.

From cotton solid:
- Fold fabric in half lengthwise right sides together, matching selvages.

  Cut 6 (24 x 18½-inch) A pocket rectangles.

  Cut 8 (18½ x 4½-inch) B spacer rectangles.
- Unfold remaining fabric to cut pieces from single thickness.

  Cut 4 additional 18½ x 4½-inch B spacer rectangles.

  Cut 1 (4½ x 9½-inch) C rectangle.

From cotton print:
- Fold fabric in half lengthwise right sides together, matching selvages.

  Cut 6 (24 x 18½-inch) A pocket rectangles.

  Cut 2 (25½ x 18½-inch) D backing rectangles.

  Cut 4 (6½ x 18½-inch) E hanger rectangles.
- Unfold remaining fabric to cut pieces from single thickness.

  Cut 2 (18½ x 4½-inch) B spacer rectangles.
- Cut 1 (4½ x 9½-inch) C rectangle.

From heavy-weight interfacing:
- Fold interfacing in half across the width.

  Cut 14 (17½ x 3½-inch) F strips.

  Cut 4 (18½ x 6½-inch) G rectangles.

  Cut 2 (9½ x 4½-inch) H rectangles. Set aside 1 H rectangle for another project.

Make It Simple!

Use a ½-inch seam allowance and 80/12 needle and stitch right sides together unless otherwise indicated. Refer to Basic Sewing Techniques for trimming seam allowances, backstitching, topstitching and echo stitching.

1. Following manufacturer's instructions, fuse interfacing H to wrong side of cotton solid C.

2. Layer print C right sides together with solid C. Using strap pattern given on pattern insert, cut six strap pieces from layered rectangles.

3. Insert ribbon between one each print and solid strap pieces for turning.

4. Using a ¼-inch seam allowance, stitch around each strap, reinforcing the seams with echo stitching. Trim seams, turn right side out using ribbon, gently pushing points out with a point turner. Press flat.

5. Mark and stitch a 1-inch-long buttonhole ¾-inch from point on each strap (Figure 1). Carefully open buttonhole and topstitch around the edge of strap.

Figure 1

6. Repeat steps 3–5 with remaining strap pieces. Set completed straps aside.

7. To make pockets, layer one each solid and print A right sides together. Stitch along both 24-inch sides to form a tube. Press seams open. Turn right side out and press tube flat. Repeat to make six pockets.

8. Determine which side of the pocket you want to show on the outside. In the sample, one solid and two print pockets are on each side. Topstitch close to stitched edges to complete the pockets. Set aside.

If you wish to embellish the pockets, follow the Make It Fancy! instructions on page 11 at this point.

9. Center interfacing F on wrong side of a solid B and fuse in place following manufacturer's instructions. Repeat for all F and solid and print B pieces. *Note: To help reduce bulk, the interfacing does not extend into the seam allowances.*

10. Follow manufacturer's instructions and step 9 to fuse interfacing G pieces to the wrong side of all E pieces.

11. Fold interfaced E pieces in half across width. Position hanger pattern, given on pattern insert, on fold (Figure 2). Trace and cut out hanger shape. Repeat to cut four hanger pieces.

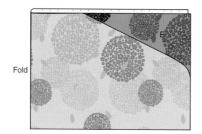

Figure 2

12. Transfer dots on hanger pattern to right side of one hanger piece for strap placement. Position and baste solid side of straps to right side of hanger piece matching raw edges. Set hanger pieces aside.

13. Center and pin the solid side of one pocket to the right side of a solid B, matching long raw edges and stitch (Figure 3a). Repeat for opposite side of pocket and B referring to Figure 3b to complete a pocket unit.

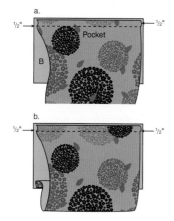

Figure 3

14. Repeat step 13 to make six pocket units.

15. Arrange three pocket units with three solid and one print B rectangles as shown in Figure 4. Stitch together as arranged and press seams toward the

top pocket. Repeat with remaining three pocket units and solid and print B rectangles to make another pocket strip.

Figure 4

16. Press ½ inch to wrong side of bottom solid B piece in pocket strip and use fabric glue to hold in place.

17. Stitch the hanger piece with straps attached to the top of one pocket strip; press seam toward hanger piece (Figure 5). Repeat with second pocket strip and a plain hanger piece to make a second pocket/hanger unit.

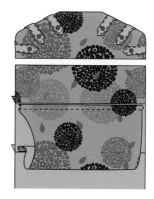

Figure 5

18. Stitch remaining hanger pieces to one short edge of each D backing rectangle to make D units; press seams toward D.

19. With pockets facing up, lay a pocket/hanger unit flat, and arrange and pin the pockets away from the outside edges as flat as possible to prevent them being caught in the seams.

20. Layer and pin a D unit on top of the pocket/hanger unit, right sides together, matching raw edges.

21. Fold ½ inch to the wrong side of the D bottom edge to match the bottom B edge of the pocket strip.

22. Stitch around the layered units, leaving the straight bottom edges open. Reinforce seams around top hanger piece using echo stitching. Grade seam allowances at curves and trim pivot points.

23. Turn right side out. Remove pins holding pockets in place. Use point turner to shape hanger piece and press flat.

24. Topstitch along seam between pocket and B pieces and then around outside edges, closing the bottom opening.

25. Repeat steps 19–24 to construct a second pocket section.

26. Layer the pocket section with the straps attached, pockets facing down, with metal or plastic hanger and the remaining pocket section, with pockets facing up.

27. Pull the straps over the hanger and mark button positions (Figure 6); stitch buttons in place. ***Note: Buttons will be located approximately 1¾ inches from the top and side edges of the hanger top edge. You may need to adjust this based on the hanger. Place the pocket sections on the hanger; if adjustments need to be made, relocate the buttons so the pockets hang straight.*** ■

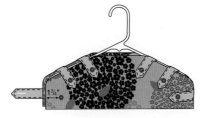

Figure 6

There's just something about a wide expanse of solid fabric that makes me want to decorate it. I chose a very subtle stitching detail for this project, but you might want to do a little more.

Take a look at the decorative stitches your machine has to offer. If you haven't tried out your decorative stitches before, now's your chance!

Create a sample for your stitching made up of the same fabric and number of thicknesses you'll be sewing through. This will give you an idea of what the stitch will look like and any adjustments which need to be made. In this case, the decorative topstitching was done through four layers of fabric.

Take the time to do a test stitch-out. Learn how the stitch is formed, such as which stitch is made first, how many times the needle moves through the stitch, and when the stitch repeats itself.

Should you ever need to restart a decorative stitch because of a broken thread or needle, skipped stitches or no bobbin thread, use the sample you made and what you learned about the stitch to help you restart. Some machines will do this automatically.

To complete this project, continue at step 9 of the Make It Simple! instructions on page 10.

ORGANIZING TIP

Keep a recycling bin near the door where you bring in the mail. Immediately sort out the junk mail into the bin before you take your mail anywhere else. Periodically go through this bin and shred documents containing personally identifying information, especially credit card offers.

The need for organization begins as soon as you enter your home. After misplacing my keys on a regular basis and forgetting to take the outgoing mail to the mailbox, I thought a perfect solution would be a tray that could hold these daily items and make my mornings stress-free.

The trays can be used individually, placed side by side, or stacked inside one another. The larger tray can be used for mail; the smaller for keys, coins or other things we tend to leave at the door. The trays can be placed on a side table, counter or ottoman.

Entryway Mail & Key Trays

Finished Sizes
Mail Tray: 15 x 12 x 2 inches
Key Tray: 6 x 6 x 2 inches

Materials
Note: Materials are for one mail tray and two key trays.

- 44/45-inch-wide woven fabrics:
    ½ yard neutral linen
    ½ yard cotton print
- ½ yard 58-inch-wide foam stabilizer
- 24 (14mm) buttons
- 12 (2mm) non-metal, ponytail elastics
- Basting spray
- Acrylic ruler with degree marks (optional)
- 1-inch-wide painter's tape (optional)
- Basic sewing supplies and equipment

Cutting
Refer to Cutting Layouts provided on pattern insert for specific cutting instructions. Trim away selvages from fabric edges before cutting pieces.

From neutral linen:
- Cut 1 (17½ x 20-inch) A rectangle.
- Cut 2 (11-inch) B squares.

From cotton print:
- Cut 1 (16½ x 19½-inch) C lining rectangle.
- Cut 2 (10½-inch) D lining squares.

From foam stabilizer:
- Cut 1 (17½ x 20-inch) A foam stabilizer rectangle.
- Cut 2 (11-inch) B foam stabilizer squares.

Make It Simple!
Use a ¼-inch seam allowance and 80/12 needle, and stitch right sides together unless otherwise

indicated. Instructions are the same for all tray sizes. Refer to Basic Sewing Techniques for grading seam allowances, backstitching and topstitching.

1. Follow basting spray manufacturer's instructions to spray-baste A and B foam stabilizer pieces to the wrong side of the corresponding A and B linen pieces.

If you wish to embellish the fabric with stitching, follow the Make It Fancy! instructions on page 15 at this point.

2. Trim basted A piece to a 16½ x 19½-inch rectangle. Trim basted B pieces to 10½-inch squares.

3. Match raw edges of basted A and C lining right sides together and pin the center of each side through all layers. Repeat with basted B and D lining pieces.

4. Draw a 2-inch square in each corner of basted A and C lining referring to Figure 1. Use scissors to cut out the marked square from both layers of each corner, referring again to Figure 1.

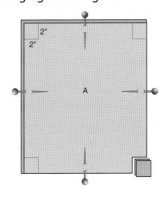

Figure 1

5. Mark a point ¼ inch from the inside cutout corner (Figure 2).

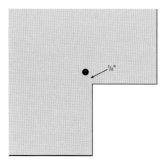

Figure 2

6. Pin and stitch around the A-C piece, leaving an opening for turning along one edge. Reinforce all corners with backstitching.

7. Reduce bulk in the corners by trimming the seam allowances on all inside and outside corners. Turn right side out through opening. Use a point turner to push out the corners and make them as square as possible. Press the tray flat.

8. At the opening, turn seam allowances ¼ inch to inside and pin.

9. Change to a 90/14 needle. With the linen facing up, topstitch completely around the tray close to the edge, making sure to catch all layers at the pinned opening.

10. Repeat steps 4–9 with B-D pieces.

11. Mark the position of the button centers ½ inch from sides of all outer corners on trays (Figure 3). Stitch buttons to each corner by hand or machine. *Note: Before attaching buttons, make and attach one elastic loop and test the fit on each tray. Relocate the buttons if the tray does not form correctly.*

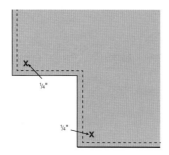

Figure 3

12. To give trays more structure, lay tray with the lining facing up. Fold and press one side of tray toward the center with a hot iron to create firm

creases. Topstitch through all layers near the edge of fold (Figure 4). Repeat on all sides.

Figure 4

13. To make the elastic loops, thread a needle with a length of thread and knot. Pinch the elastic loop in the center to form a figure-8 shape (Figure 5). Create a loop with thread around the center of the elastic loop by inserting the needle between the knotted threads, referring again to Figure 5.

Figure 5

14. Pull thread tightly and wrap the thread around the loop 6–8 times. Tie off, burying threads in the elastic loop and clipping close to the loop. Repeat for all 12 loops.

15. Wrap the loops around the buttons to form the sides of trays.

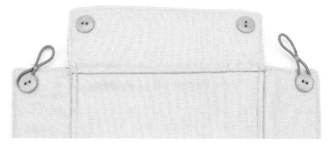

16. When not in use, the trays can be stored flat or nested together. ∎

Linen is a beautiful fabric on its own, but you may want to create a bit more texture before finishing this project. This technique shows you how to create a 60-degree diamond grid on your fabric.

1. Using a large acrylic ruler, align the 60-degree line with the lower edge of the exterior fabric, slightly away from a corner.

2. Tear a long piece of 1-inch wide painter's tape and align it along the edge of the ruler on the fabric (Figure 6).

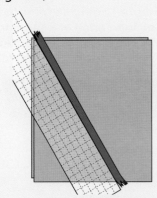

Figure 6

3. Topstitch through all layers next to the masking tape on either side, being careful not to stitch through the tape.

4. Move the tape to the side of one stitched line and topstitch next to the tape, creating lines spaced 1 inch apart across fabric (Figure 7). Repeat until entire piece is stitched.

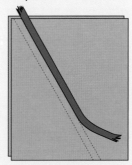

Figure 7

5. Rotate fabric 90 degrees from where you started stitching. This time, align the 45-degree line with the lower edge of fabric, slightly away from the corner. Position the tape and repeat step 3 referring to Figure 8 to stitch across the fabric.

Figure 8

To complete the project, continue at step 2 of Make It Simple! on page 13.

Throw pillows are fairly ubiquitous in homes these days, especially if there's also a sewing machine nearby. Pillow covers are a quick and easy way to spruce up a home's decor, but it's even better when those pillows can do double duty!

For those moments when you need to quickly clean and organize, the pockets make a good place to quickly stash remote controls, magazines, writing implements and any other small object that seems to gravitate to flat and empty surfaces.

Stowaway Pillow Cover

Finished Size
Pillow: 12 x 16 inches

Materials
- ½ yard 44/45-inch-wide microsuede
- 14-inch zipper
- 12 x 16-inch pillow form
- Make It Fancy! option:
    2 (20 x 22-inch) peacock blue bamboo
    or wool felt
    2 (20 x 22-inch) raspberry bamboo
    or wool felt
- Basic sewing supplies and equipment

Cutting
Refer to Cutting Layouts provided on pattern insert for specific cutting instructions. Trim away selvages from microsuede before cutting pieces.

From microsuede:
- Cut 2 (13 x 17-inch) A pillow rectangles.
- Cut 1 (7½ x 17-inch) B pocket rectangle.

From bamboo or wool felt
(Make It Fancy! option):
- Use 2-inch circle pattern on pattern insert to cut approximately 300 (2-inch) C circles. *Note: Cutting 300 circles by hand can make this embellishment time consuming and painful. If you have a die-cutting machine, now is a good time to use it!*

Make It Simple!
Use a ½-inch seam allowance and 80/12 needle and stitch right sides together unless otherwise indicated. Refer to Basic Sewing Techniques for trimming seam allowances, backstitching, bar tacks and topstitching.

1. Referring to Figure 1, fold and press ¼ inch to wrong side of one long edge of B twice to make a double-turned ¼-inch hem. Topstitch close to folded edge.

Figure 1

2. On the right side of B, mark a pocket stitching line 4½ inches from each short side.

3. Layer B, right side up, on right side of one A rectangle, aligning bottom raw edges and baste. Stitch on pocket stitching lines (Figure 2), backstitching at upper edge of pocket. Set aside.

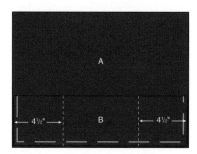

Figure 2

4. Finish raw edges of both A rectangles with a zigzag or over-edge stitch, or serger.

If you wish to embellish the pillow, follow the Make It Fancy! instructions on page 19 at this point.

5. Match the bottom edges of the A rectangles and pin. Stitch from outside edges toward center 2 inches referring to Figure 3.

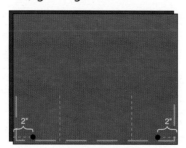

Figure 3

6. Open zipper and pin to one side of seam allowance with zipper stop and pull at end of 2-inch stitching and teeth toward seam opening. Stitch one side of zipper to seam allowance using zipper foot to stitch close to zipper teeth (Figure 4a).

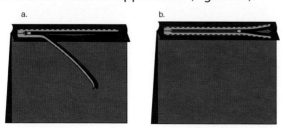

Figure 4

7. Partially close zipper and repeat step 6 on opposite seam allowance referring to Figure 4b.

When close to zipper pull, stop stitching and cut threads. Completely open zipper and finish stitching zipper.

8. Stitch a bar tack at both ends of the zipper opening by hand or machine (Figure 5).

Figure 5

9. Stitch around the remaining sides of pillow, reinforcing corners (Figure 6). Trim corners and turn right side out. Push out corners with point turner.

Figure 6

10. Insert pillow form and close zipper. ∎

Bamboo felt gives this pillow a very luxurious feel and creates a wonderful texture across the surface. An added bonus is that felt does not fray, so this pillow will look great for years.

1. Mark a 1½-inch perimeter around the right side of the exterior piece without the pocket (Figure 7). *Note: Try to keep embellishments inside this perimeter.*

1½"

Figure 7

2. Draw a curvy line inside the perimeter with fabric marker to use as a guideline for stitching embellishments, referring again to Figure 7.

3. Position a peacock blue circle near the end of this curvy line and the edge of the perimeter; tack the center of the circle to the fabric (Figure 8).

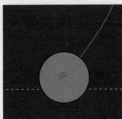

Figure 8

4. Lift up one side of the circle you just stitched in place. Place another blue circle next to it, following the curvy line. Tack the circle to the fabric.

5. Repeat for the third circle. Try not to stitch circles too close together—they should start to appear like wide taco shells (Figure 9).

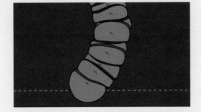

Figure 9

6. Continue stitching blue circles along the curvy line until you reach the opposite perimeter line. *Note: The first row will have approximately 15–20 circles.*

7. For the next row, work on one side of the blue circles, lifting up the sides of two circles and placing a raspberry circle next to them (Figure 10).

Figure 10

8. Continue stitching circles in this manner, alternating colors as you complete each row. As you complete more rows, the circles will start to look like ruffles.

The key to this technique is to not place the circles too close together or too far apart. Use leftover microsuede and some of your felt circles to practice achieving the right density—approximately 10–12 circles per additional row works well. If you want to relocate a circle, simply cut the tack and move it.

To complete this project, continue at step 5 of Make It Simple! instructions on page 18.

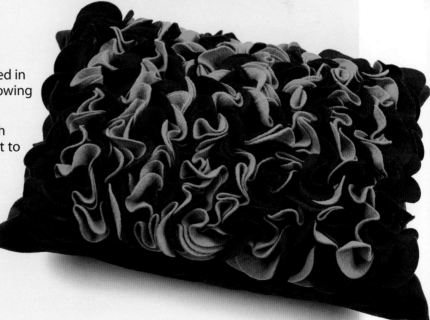

I refer to my dining room as my "Room of Sanity." No matter what else is going on in the house or how busy I am, I keep my dining room table clean at all times. That way, I always have a spot to retreat to for meals or when I need a quiet place to work. My office desk is another story!

Keeping the table clean doesn't mean there's nothing on it, and I don't mind leaving items on the table when they are great decorative objects like these boxes. Make a casual set for everyday dining, and something a little more elegant for larger parties.

Napkin & Utensil Boxes

Finished Size
Napkin or Utensil Box: 7 x 9 x 3 inches

Materials
- 44/45-inch-wide woven fabric:
  - ½ yard cotton or linen
  - ⅔ yard cotton print
- ¼ yard 45-inch-wide heavy-weight fusible interfacing
- ⅜ yard 58-inch-wide foam stabilizer
- #5 pearl cotton or Sashiko thread
- Fabric-glue stick
- Couching or open-toe sewing machine presser foot (optional)
- Basic sewing supplies and equipment

Cutting
Refer to Cutting Layouts provided on pattern insert for specific cutting instructions. Trim away selvages on fabric before cutting pieces

From cotton or linen:
- Cut 2 (13 x 15-inch) A exterior rectangles.
  Make It Fancy! Option: Cut 2 (14 x 16-inch) A exterior rectangles.

From cotton print:
- Cut 2 (13 x 15-inch) C lining rectangles.
- Cut 1 (10 x 16-inch) D utensil divider rectangle.
- Cut 1 (8 x 14-inch) E napkin divider rectangle.

From heavy-weight fusible interfacing:
- Cut 2 (7 x 9-inch) F rectangles.
- Cut 1 (9 x 15-inch) G rectangle.
- Cut 1 (7 x 13-inch) H rectangle.

From foam stabilizer:
- Cut 2 (13 x 15-inch) I rectangles.

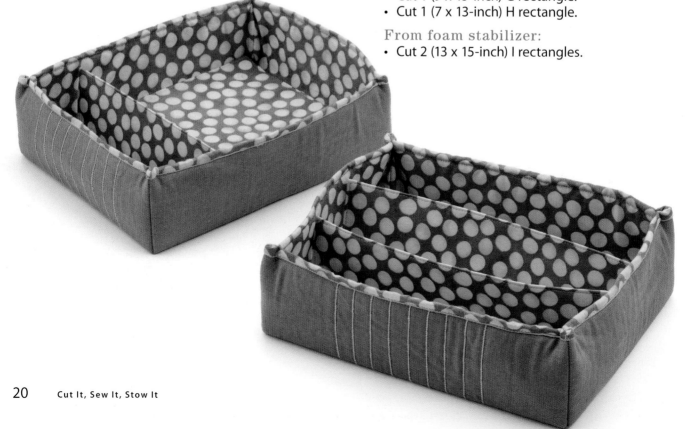

ORGANIZING TIP

If you have a hard time keeping the dining room from becoming a landing zone for junk, consider setting the table. A nice tablecloth and place settings will discourage you from disturbing the peaceful scene with loose papers or other clutter.

Make It Simple!

Use a ¼-inch seam allowance and 80/12 needle and stitch right sides together unless otherwise indicated. Refer to Basic Sewing Techniques for trimming seam allowances, backstitching, topstitching and bar tacks.

Completing the Dividers

1. Center interfacing F pieces on wrong side of B (divider bottoms) and fuse following manufacturer's instructions. Repeat with interfacing G on D (utensil divider) and interfacing H on E (napkin divider).

2. On all pieces, press raw edges to wrong side along edge of interfacing (Figure 1). Use glue stick to temporarily hold fabric in place instead of pins.

Figure 1

3. Mark lines 7 and 11 inches from one 8-inch edge on wrong side of napkin divider. Fold and press with right sides together on marked lines; allow to cool.

4. Fold the napkin divider wrong sides together so the two previous folds meet, creating a divider flap (Figure 2). Press and allow to cool.

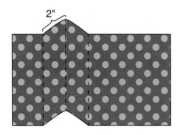

Figure 2   **Figure 3**

5. Topstitch the flap along the sides and top edge to secure referring to Figure 3.

6. Layer and pin napkin divider wrong sides together with divider bottom, matching edges. Topstitch on each side of the divider flap, close to the fold and along the edges; stitch a 7-inch square on one side (Figure 4a), and a 2 x 7-inch rectangle on the other (Figure 4b). Set aside the divider flap insert.

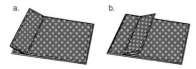

Figure 4

7. Mark lines at 2½, 6½, 8½ and 12½ inches from one 10-inch edge on wrong side of utensil divider. Fold and press right sides together on marked lines; allow to cool.

8. Fold the utensil divider right sides together on marked lines matching the 2½- and 6½-inch lines and the 8½- and 12½-inch lines creating a divider with two flaps (Figure 5).

Figure 5

9. Repeat steps 5 and 6 to topstitch the divider creating a 2 x 9-inch rectangle in the middle and two 2½ x 9-inch rectangles on the sides.

If you wish to embellish the exterior of your boxes, follow the Make It Fancy! instructions on page 23 at this point.

Completing the Box

1. Baste foam stabilizer I pieces to cotton or linen exterior rectangles.

2. Mark lines 2½ inches from all sides of the stabilized exterior rectangles on the wrong side (Figure 6). Stitch on the lines to mark the bottom and sides of the box.

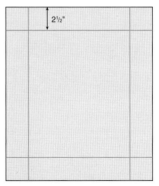

Figure 6

3. To form the sides of the box, fold each corner so that the diagonals meet with right sides together and stitch along the marked line; trim seam allowance to ¼ inch (Figure 7). Repeat with all four corners. Do not turn box right side out.

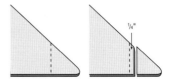

Figure 7

4. Repeat steps 11 and 12 using C (lining rectangles) and skipping the stitching in step 11. Turn lining right side out.

5. Insert lining into exterior box, right sides facing and matching corners. Pin top edges together, leaving an opening for turning on one end; stitch (Figure 8).

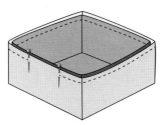

Figure 8

6. Trim the seam allowance to approximately ⅛ inch except at the opening (Figure 9).

Figure 9

7. Turn the box right side out through the opening. Press the lining away from the exterior around the box. Turn the opening seam allowances to the inside and pin.

8. Insert the lining into the box, allowing the lining to peek out above the box.

9. Change sewing machine needle to size 90/14.

10. From the right side of the box, topstitch all around the box where the lining seam and exterior meet to create a faux piping and close the opening. *Note: If you opted for the Make It Fancy! embellishment, couch pearl cotton when topstitching as well.*

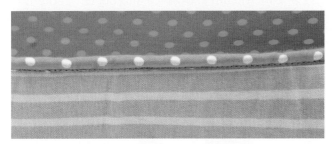

11. To give the sides more stability and give the box more interest, press the sides together at one corner; bar-tack near the corner in the seam. Repeat on all four corners.

12. Repeat steps 1–12 to make second box. Insert a divider into each box. ■

MAKE IT FANCY! EMBELLISHING

If you've never couched threads before, you're in for a treat! This technique is a fast and simple way to add interest and 3-D texture to a fabric. Couching will sometimes cause the fabric to draw up slightly, so it's better to start with a larger piece than you need so that you can trim it to size after couching.

1. Mark a horizontal or vertical line down the center of the right side of one 14 x 16-inch exterior piece. Mark four additional lines spaced ½ inch apart on either side of the centerline.

2. Set sewing machine to a short, narrow zigzag stitch (approximately 2mm wide and 2mm long).

3. Using an open-toe or couching foot, insert a length of pearl cotton on top of the center marked line and centered underneath the needle and the presser foot. Extend the pearl cotton 2–3 inches behind the presser foot so you can hang onto it when you start stitching.

4. Stitch over the pearl cotton, making sure that the zigzag stitch does not catch the pearl cotton. Do not tug on the pearl cotton but keep it centered over the marked line. Stitch to the opposite edge and trim the pearl cotton even with the fabric edge.

5. Repeat to embellish along each marked line.

6. When couching is complete, trim the exterior fabric to 13 x 15 inches.

To complete this project, continue at step 1 of Completing the Box of Make It Simple! instructions on page 22.

I was brainstorming with a friend of mine one day and she said, "You should design a cute way to store plastic grocery bags. Everything on the market is so ugly." That's how I first started thinking about this project.

On a practical note, I am one of those people who own an ugly bag container. I currently store my plastic bags in an empty tissue box, which was the inspiration behind the final design.

Plastic Bag Hamper

Finished Size
9½ x 7 x 5½ inches

Materials
- 44/45-inch-wide woven fabric:
    ½ yard cotton novelty print
    ¾ yard cotton solid
- 12-inch square cotton print
- 7½ x 10-inch piece heavy-weight fusible interfacing
- ⅓ yard 45-inch-wide fusible fleece
- 2 (12 x 18-inch) sheets ultra-stiff 7-count plastic canvas
- #8 white pearl cotton
- Large-eye embroidery needle
- 1 yard ⅜-inch-wide satin ribbon
- 2 (1-inch) novelty buttons
- Seam sealant
- Basic sewing supplies and equipment

Cutting

From cotton novelty print:
Novelty prints tend to be directional. The Cutting Layout is based on the orientation of the print. You may need to plan for more fabric if your print runs in the opposite direction. Trim away selvages on fabric before cutting pieces

- Cut 1 (10¼ x 15½-inch) hamper back A rectangle.
- Cut 2 (10¼ x 3¼-inch) hamper side B rectangles.
- Cut 1 (10¼ x 10-inch) hamper front C rectangle.
    Cut hamper front before hamper bottom.
- Cut 1 (3¼ x 10¼-inch) hamper bottom front E.
- Cut 1 (4½ x 31-inch) drawstring lining D rectangle.

From cotton solid:
- Cut 2 (10¼ x 15½-inch) lining A rectangles.
- Cut 1 (10¼ x 10-inch) pocket lining C rectangle.
- Cut 1 (10¼ x 7½-inch) pocket front F rectangle.
    Make It Fancy! Option: Cut 1 (14½ x 7½-inch) pocket front rectangle.
- Cut 1 (6 x 31-inch) drawstring G rectangle.
- Cut 2 (4 x 9½-inch) handle H rectangles.

From fusible fleece:
- Cut 2 (10¼ x 15½-inch) A rectangles.

From 7-count plastic canvas:
- Plastic canvas should only be cut with sharp craft scissors (not sewing shears). Mark the cutting lines first with permanent marker, and then cut by hand with scissors.
- Cut 2 (9¼ x 6¼-inch) front/back I rectangles from sheet 1.
- Cut 2 (6¼ x 5¼-inch) side J rectangles from sheet 2.
- Cut 1 (9¼ x 5¼-inch) bottom K rectangle from remainder of 2nd sheet.

Make It Simple!
Use a ¼-inch seam allowance and 80/12 needle and stitch right sides together unless otherwise indicated. Refer to Basic Sewing Techniques for trimming, backstitching, echo stitching and topstitching.

1. Fold the cotton print 12-inch square in half along one diagonal. Fold in half again along second diagonal referring to Figure 1.

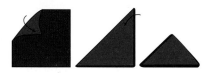

Figure 1

2. Rotate the folded fabric so that the open fold is on the left and the raw edges are closest to you. Cut off the double fold on the left (Figure 2). Cut 2½-inch strips across the remaining width referring again to Figure 2 to cut two each long, medium and short bias strips. Set aside one long strip.

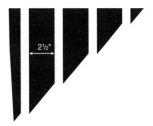

Figure 2

3. Stitch the remaining strips together using a diagonal seam to make one long strip approximately 39 inches long (Figure 3); press seams open. On one short end, turn ¼ inch to wrong side.

Figure 3

4. Fold and press strip in half lengthwise (Figure 4). Open flat, fold and press both long raw edges to middle crease. Refold and press in half lengthwise again. Set aside for binding top edge of hamper.

Figure 4

5. Repeat step 4 with long strip that was set aside in step 2. Set aside for pocket binding.

6. Layer drawstring and drawstring lining right sides together. Stitch one long side; press seam open. On short sides, press ¼ inch to wrong side and topstitch close to edge to complete drawstring top.

7. Align raw edges of drawstring top wrong sides together; press. Topstitch along the seam where the drawstring and drawstring lining meet to form the casing for the drawstring ribbon (Figure 5).

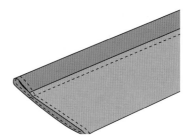

Figure 5

8. Fold drawstring top in half lengthwise novelty print sides together and stitch short side, stopping at the edge of the casing to complete the drawstring top. Set aside.

9. Fold one handle in half lengthwise; press the fold. Unfold flat and press long raw edges to the center. Refold in half lengthwise and press handle flat.

10. Topstitch ¼ inch from each edge and down center of the handle (Figure 6). Repeat for both handles.

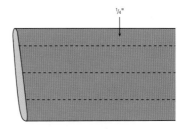

Figure 6

11. Follow manufacturer's instructions to fuse 7½ x 10-inch heavy-weight fusible interfacing to F (pocket front).

If you wish to embellish the pocket of your hamper, follow the Make It Fancy! instructions on page 28 at this point.

12. Stitch E (hamper bottom front) to bottom edge of pocket front F. Press seam toward bottom front.

13. Baste pocket lining to pocket front, wrong sides together, around sides and bottom to make pocket unit.

14. Align straight edge of pocket curve trimming template, located on the pattern insert, with raw edges at pocket unit top and trace along curved line; cut through all layers on traced line (Figure 7).

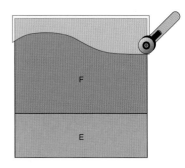

Figure 7

15. Insert curved edge of pocket unit between folds of pocket binding; pin, easing the binding around the curves (Figure 8). Topstitch binding to pocket close to binding lower edge; trim binding even with raw edges of pocket.

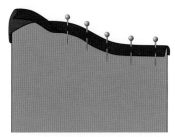

Figure 8

16. Layer pocket on right side of hamper front, aligning raw edges along sides and bottom; baste.

17. Mark a line 5 inches from long edge of hamper front.

18. Pin hamper side pieces to pocket front. Stitch through all layers; press seams toward hamper sides (Figure 9).

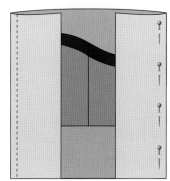

Figure 9

19. Topstitch lower seam of pocket and along marked line to divide pocket, backstitching at top edge of pocket.

20. Follow manufacturer's instructions to apply fusible fleece A pieces to pocket assembly and hamper back wrong side.

21. Fold handle in half and then pin and baste to side of pocket assembly, 1½ inches from top edge (Figure 10). Repeat for remaining handle.

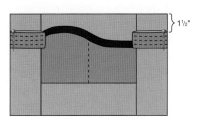

1½"

Figure 10

22. Layer exterior pieces right sides together and pin around sides and bottom, making sure handles are inside. Change to a 90/14 size needle. Stitch sides and bottom of hamper and press seams open. Repeat for lining pieces.

23. To box corners, align side and bottom seam of hamper exterior. Stitch across folded corner 2½ inches from point; trim seam allowance to ¼ inch (Figure 11). Repeat for all exterior and lining corners.

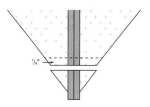

¼"

Figure 11

24. Turn hamper exterior right side out. Fold hamper at corners with wrong sides together; press. Topstitch close to corner folds.

25. Flatten and center the handle on the hamper side and pin in place. Topstitch handle ends close to folds. Echo-stitch to reinforce the seam.

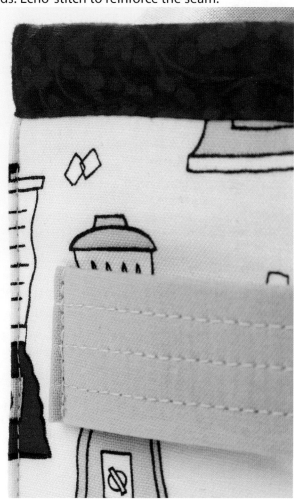

26. Lay out plastic canvas pieces like a flattened box. Use the pearl cotton to loosely whipstitch the pieces of mesh together (Figure 12). *Note: These stitches should be loose enough so that each piece can move freely without the edges touching.*

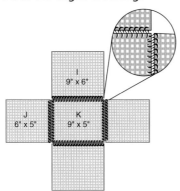

Figure 12

27. Insert mesh sections into hamper exterior. Use pearl cotton to anchor mesh sides to side seam allowances.

28. Insert lining into hamper, over mesh. Pin and baste lining to exterior, matching side seams and distributing the lining evenly around the box.

29. Insert and pin drawstring top into hamper with the novelty fabric facing up, centering seam over front pocket and matching raw edges. Baste.

30. Starting with the folded-under edge of binding about 5 inches from end, insert top edge of hamper between folds of binding and pin around box (Figure 13).

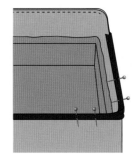

Figure 13

31. When you get within 5 inches of starting end, overlap and pin the ends together, unfolding binding as you go. Topstitch along the beginning folded edge where the binding meets by hand or machine. Trim excess binding strip close to seam.

32. Finish pinning binding to hamper. Topstitch binding to hamper through all layers. *Note: The mesh should be flexible enough to allow you to maneuver the hamper under your needle.*

33. Thread ribbon through the casing and the novelty buttons. Cut the ends of the ribbon at an angle, knot and clip close to the knot. Apply seam sealant on ribbon ends to keep them from unraveling. ∎

MAKE IT FANCY! EMBELLISHING

If your sewing machine allows you to stitch with a twin needle, odds are it also has an accessory presser foot attachment for pintucking. A pintuck is simply a double row of parallel lines that make a slightly raised texture using a special presser foot. The foot has grooves along the bottom that allow you to control the spacing of the pintucks and keep them from getting crushed.

There's just enough pintucking on this project to give you an idea of whether or not you'll like it!

1. On the right side of pocket front, mark a line 4½ inches from left edge.

2. If your machine has an attachment for pintucks, refer to your machine's manual for instructions on using the pintuck attachment and twin-needle sewing.

3. Stitch 15–20 pintucks between the left edge and the marked line, approximately ½ inch apart.

4. If your machine does not have a pintuck attachment, simply choose another stitch that can be done with a twin needle as a decorative element.

5. Loosen the top tension slightly. This imbalance in the tension will draw the top threads to the bottom and cause a slight pucker, which will mimic a pintuck.

To complete this project, continue at step 12 of Make It Simple! instructions on page 26.

Save time getting dressed in the morning, or get organized and packed for a trip in no time with this accessory hanger. This hanger comes in two sizes—for both adult- and kid-size hangers—so you can make one for every member of the family, or every day of the week!

Accessory Hanger

Finished Size

Child's Hanger: 10 x 14 inches
Adult's Hanger: 14 x 14 inches

Materials

For Child's Hanger:

- 35 (2½-inch) squares assorted cotton solids or prints
- ⅓ yard 44/45-inch-wide cotton print
- ⅓ yard 44/45-inch-wide heavy-weight fusible interfacing
- 10½ x 14½-inch rectangle fusible fleece
- ⅓ yard 18-inch-wide clear vinyl
- 5 (½-inch) snaps
- 10-inch zipper
- 1 child's size hanger
- Basic sewing supplies and equipment

For Adult's Hanger:

- 49 (2½-inch) squares assorted cotton solids or prints
- ½ yard 44/45-inch-wide cotton print
- ½ yard 44/45-inch-wide heavy-weight fusible interfacing
- 14½-inch square fusible fleece
- ⅓ yard 18-inch-wide clear vinyl
- 7 (½-inch) snaps
- 14-inch zipper
- 1 standard hanger
- Basic sewing supplies and equipment

Cutting for Child's Hanger

Refer to Cutting Layouts provided on pattern insert for specific cutting instructions. Trim away selvages on fabric before cutting pieces.

From cotton print:

- Cut 4 (2 x 10½-inch) zipper binding A rectangles.
- Cut 2 (5 x 10½-inch) snap panel B rectangles.
- Cut 2 (2½ x 10½-inch) C finishing strips.
- Cut 1 (10½ x 14½-inch) backing D rectangle.
- Cut 1 (2½ x 6-inch) pocket flap E rectangle.
- Cut 1 (2½ x 4-inch) pocket flap F rectangle.

From heavy-weight fusible interfacing:

- Cut 2 (4½ x 10½-inch) interfacing B rectangles.
- Cut 1 (10½ x 14½-inch) interfacing D rectangle.
- Cut 1 (2½ x 6-inch) interfacing E rectangle.
- Cut 1 (2½ x 4-inch) interfacing F rectangle.
- Cut 4 (¾ x 10½-inch) interfacing G rectangles.

From clear vinyl:

- Cut 1 (5¼ x 10½-inch) pocket I rectangle.
- Cut 1 (6 x 10½-inch) pocket H rectangle.

Cutting for Adult's Hanger

Refer to Cutting Layouts provided on pattern insert for specific cutting instructions.

From cotton print:

- Cut 4 (2 x 14½-inch) zipper binding A rectangles.
- Cut 2 (5 x 14½-inch) snap panel B rectangles.
- Cut 2 (2½ x 14½-inch) C finishing strips.
- Cut 1 (14½-inch) backing D square.
- Cut 1 (2½ x 6-inch) pocket flap E rectangle.
- Cut 2 (2½ x 4-inch) pocket flap F rectangles.

From heavy-weight fusible interfacing:

- Cut 2 (4½ x 14½-inch) interfacing B rectangles.
- Cut 1 (14½-inch) interfacing D square.
- Cut 1 (2½ x 6-inch) interfacing E rectangle.
- Cut 2 (2½ x 4-inch) interfacing F rectangles.
- Cut 4 (¾ x 14½-inch) interfacing G rectangles.

From clear vinyl:

- Cut 1 (5¼ x 14½-inch) pocket I rectangle.
- Cut 1 (6 x 14½-inch) pocket H rectangle.

Make It Simple!

Instructions are the same for both adult's and child's hangers unless noted. Adult's hanger measurements or totals are listed in parentheses. Use a ¼-inch seam allowance and 80/12 needle unless otherwise indicated. Refer to Basic Sewing Techniques for trimming, echo stitching, back-stitching, bar tack and topstitching.

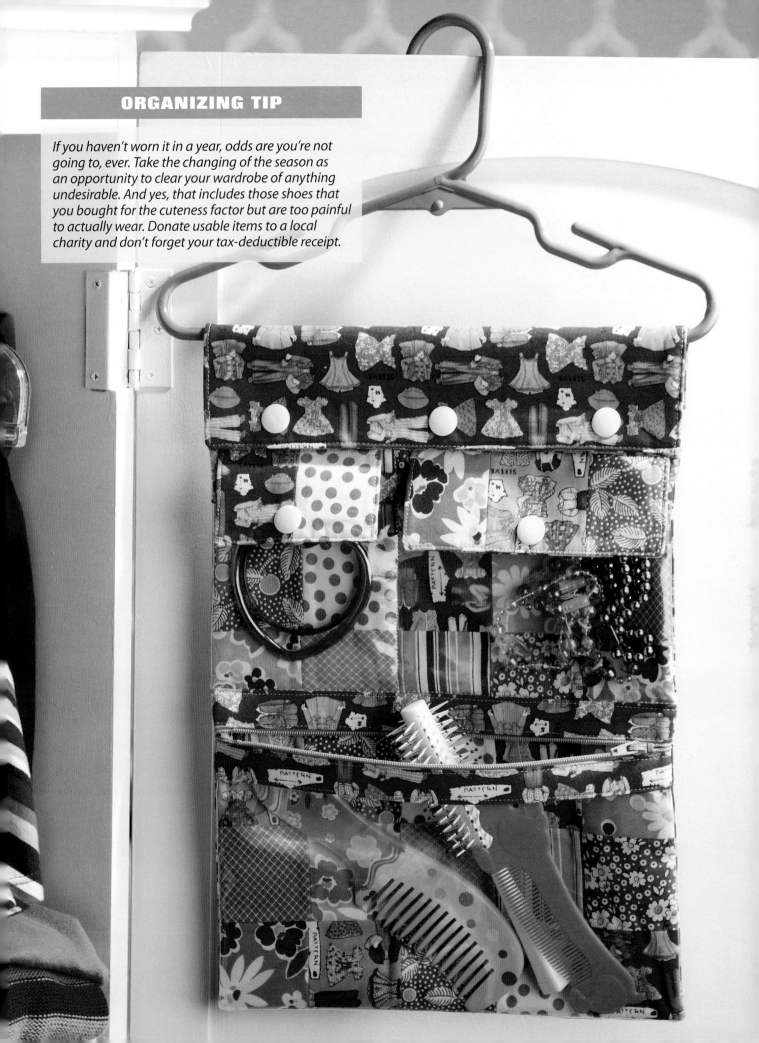

ORGANIZING TIP

If you haven't worn it in a year, odds are you're not going to, ever. Take the changing of the season as an opportunity to clear your wardrobe of anything undesirable. And yes, that includes those shoes that you bought for the cuteness factor but are too painful to actually wear. Donate usable items to a local charity and don't forget your tax-deductible receipt.

1. Center and fuse an interfacing G on wrong side of each zipper binding A following manufacturer's instructions.

2. Fold sides of zipper binding over to enclose the interfacing referring to Figure 1. Use glue stick and a hot iron to temporarily hold the binding edge in place. Repeat for all zipper binding strips.

Figure 1

3. Sandwich vinyl pocket I between two zipper binding strips, matching top edges (Figure 2). Clip binding strips to top pocket edge to hold temporarily.

Figure 2

TIP

Be careful not to pierce vinyl with pins. Pins will leave permanent holes in the vinyl. Use fabric glue or paper clips to hold vinyl pieces in place during construction.

4. Edgestitch lower edge of zipper binding through both binding strips and pocket. Repeat steps 3 and 4 for vinyl pocket H.

5. Fold back the zipper binding and trim the vinyl close to the seam to reduce bulk and create a space to insert the zipper. Repeat for remaining vinyl pocket.

6. Insert and pin one side of the zipper between zipper binding strips on pocket H with the zipper pull to the left and keeping the raw edges even on the zipper tab end (Figure 3).

Figure 3

7. Topstitch the zipper to the binding, opening or closing the zipper as needed to avoid the zipper pull.

8. Repeat steps 6 and 7 to attach pocket I to the opposite side of the zipper.

9. If necessary, shorten your zipper by stitching a bar tack across the zipper teeth approximately ½ inch from raw edge. Trim zipper even with raw edge of pocket.

10. Fold one finishing strip C in half lengthwise and press. Open the strip and press long raw edges to the center. Refold and press along center fold to make pocket binding.

11. Insert upper edge of pocket I between folds of pocket binding. Pin or clip trim to top edge, being careful not to pierce the vinyl below the binding. Topstitch trim to pocket close to bottom edge (Figure 4).

Figure 4

12. Choose three 2½-inch assorted cotton solid or print squares; stitch together end to end and press seams open.

13. Trim to 6 inches long, removing ¼ inch from each end. Fuse interfacing E to pieced strip following manufacturer's instructions.

14. Choose two more 2½-inch squares and stitch together end to end; press seams open. Trim to 4 inches long, removing ¼ inch from each end. Fuse interfacing F to pieced strip following manufacturer's instructions. (Repeat for a second pocket flap F for adult's size.)

15. Layer pocket flap E and pocket flap F right sides together over the corresponding patchwork pieces from steps 12–14.

If you wish to embellish the pocket flaps by rounding the corners, follow the Make It Fancy! instructions on page 35 at this point and then continue at step 16.

16. Stitch around 3 edges of pocket flaps, reinforcing corners with echo stitching; trim corners. Turn pocket flaps right side out; press. Topstitch around the edge of the pocket flap.

17. Arrange 30 (42) 2½-inch squares for the main patchwork panel in 6 rows of 5 (7) squares. Stitch the squares together in rows; press seams open. Stitch rows together matching seams; press seams open (Figure 5 shows child's size).

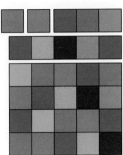

Figure 5

18. Follow manufacturer's instructions to apply fusible fleece rectangle (square) to wrong side of patchwork panel, aligning lower and side edges. *Note: 2¼ inches of fleece will be exposed at top edge.*

19. Topstitch along seams of squares to further secure fleece to patchwork panel or stitch-in-the-ditch of all seams.

20. To mark the position for the pocket flap snaps, layer vinyl pocket panel over patchwork panel, aligning lower edges. Position the male snap on top of the seam between the first and second squares, with the snap just below the pocket binding referring to Figure 6. Mark with marker through the hole of the male snap on the vinyl. Repeat on the center of the fourth square. (For the adult's hanger, repeat once more between the sixth and seventh squares.)

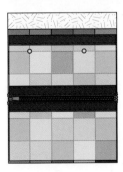

Figure 6

21. Cut a small hole in the vinyl at the marked positions. Follow the manufacturer's instructions to install the male snap on the vinyl.

22. Reposition and pin the vinyl pocket panel to the patchwork panel at the zipper section. Baste around three sides leaving the snap edge open.

23. Pin and baste the pocket flaps to the patchwork panel, patchwork side up, matching raw edges of the flaps with the exterior fabric and aligning the center seams of the squares.

24. Pin and stitch a C finishing strip to the pocket flaps (Figure 7). Press finishing strip toward the fusible fleece and fuse together.

Figure 7

25. To position the female portion of the snap, lay the flap over the male portion of the snap, and mark the center of the snap on the flap fabric. Cut a small hole where you marked and follow manufacturer's instructions to install the female snap to each pocket flap.

26. On the finishing strip, mark male portion of snap position ½ inch from seam, and 1½ inches from each side. Mark a third snap position 5¼ inches from the left edge. (On adult's hanger, mark a fourth snap 5¼ inches from the right edge.)

27. Cut a small hole through all layers at marks and follow the manufacturer's instructions to install the male snaps on the finishing strip.

28. Fuse interfacing D to the wrong side of backing following manufacturer's instructions. Pin or clip backing to patchwork panel right sides together, being careful not to pierce the vinyl with pins.

If you wish to embellish the patchwork panel by rounding the corners, follow the Make It Fancy! instructions on page 35 at this point.

29. Stitch backing to patchwork panel around three sides, leaving snap side open. Echo-stitch and trim corners. Turn right side out and press from the backing side, being careful not to apply too much heat or to touch the vinyl with the iron.

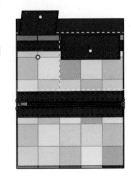

30. Change machine sewing needle to size 90/14 and topstitch along the finishing strip seam through all layers referring to white stitching on Figure 8.

Figure 8

31. To make the lower pocket, topstitch through all layers just above the upper zipper binding strip referring again to Figure 8 white stitching.

32. To make the upper pockets, topstitch on top of the vinyl, through all layers, between the second and third patchwork squares from the pocket binding edge to the top of the zipper binding.

Backstitch at the pocket binding edge referring again to Figure 8 white stitching. (On adult's hanger, repeat this step between the fifth and sixth patchwork squares.)

33. Fuse interfacing B to the wrong side of snap panel, aligning raw edges on three sides leaving ½ inch of fabric with no interfacing.

34. Press fabric ½ inch to wrong side over the interfacing. Use a glue stick and a hot iron to hold in place.

35. Repeat steps 33 and 34 with remaining snap panel and interfacing B. Pin snap panel pieces together matching raw and folded edges.

If you wish to embellish the snap panel by rounding the corners, follow the Make It Fancy! instructions at right at this point.

36. Stitch three raw edges of snap panel, echo-stitching corners (Figure 9); trim. Turn snap panel right side out; press.

Figure 9

37. Insert upper raw edge of patchwork panel between folded edges of snap panel. Pin together ¼ inch above the snaps. Topstitch completely around snap panel to secure (Figure 10).

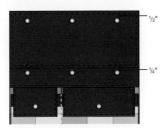

Figure 10

38. Fold the snap panel around a hanger. Position snaps ½ inch from outside edge of panel referring again to Figure 10, mark and apply female snaps as for the pocket flaps following the manufacturer's instructions.

39. Snap the panel onto a hanger. ■

MAKE IT FANCY! EMBELLISHING

Rounding corners is an easy way to add a bit of interest to an edge and can often look nicer than a squared corner, especially if you have a very thick project where a perfectly square corner is hard to achieve. To add even more interest, round just one side of the edge and leave the other square.

To round the corners, use the 2½-inch circle template from pattern insert. Align the circle in the corner you want to round off, making sure the edges of the circle touch two edges of your piece.

Mark the outside curve of the circle and carefully cut through all layers.

To complete this project, continue at step 16 or 29 of Make It Simple! instructions on page 33.

ORGANIZING TIP

Keep a pen and notebook handy near your bed. It's great for jotting down those late-night thoughts that could keep you awake, and for capturing dreams and ideas when you first wake in the morning. Writing is a great way to decompress and organize your thoughts. Once you can think clearly, you have more brain space to devote to other things that are important to you.

I don't have bedside tables in my bedroom, so these saddlebags are an essential part of keeping my bedroom neat and organized and my small nighttime items close at hand. I keep a small pack of tissues, lip balm, pen, paper, a couple of books, my journal and my Kindle there.

Bedside Saddlebag

Finished Size
17½ x 16 inches

Materials
- 44/45-inch-wide-woven fabric:
    2½ yards linen
    ¼ yard cotton print
- 1 yard 58-inch-wide foam stabilizer
- 1 yard 45-inch-wide heavy-weight fusible interfacing
- ½ yard 45-inch-wide fusible fleece
- 2 (4-yard) pieces 1-inch-wide poly webbing
- 8 (1-inch) D-rings
- Make It Fancy! option:
    ¾ yard 44/45-inch-wide cotton print
    ¼ yard 45-inch-wide fusible grid
    Perfect Pleater™
- Seam sealant
- Basic sewing supplies and equipment

Cutting
Refer to Cutting Layouts provided on pattern insert for specific cutting instructions. Trim away selvages on fabric before cutting pieces.

From linen:
- Cut 4 (18½ x 33-inch) exterior A rectangles.
- Cut 1 (4 x 24-inch) strap B rectangle.
- Cut 4 (1½ x 8½-inch) large pocket border C rectangles.
- Cut 8 (1½ x 4-inch) medium pocket border D rectangles.
- Cut 4 (4-inch) small pocket backing E squares.
- Cut 4 (3½ x 8½-inch) large pocket accordion F rectangles.
- Cut 8 (3½ x 4½-inch) medium pocket accordion G rectangles.
- Cut 2 (8½ x 14½-inch) large pocket backing H rectangles.
- Cut 4 (10 x 4½-inch) medium pocket backing I rectangles.

From cotton print:
- Cut 2 (6½ x 8½-inch) large pocket center J rectangles.
    Make It Fancy! Option:
    Cut 2 (9 x 27-inch) large pocket center J rectangles.
- Cut 4 (2½ x 4-inch) medium pocket center K rectangles.
    Make It Fancy! Option:
    Cut 2 (9 x 15-inch) medium pocket center K rectangles.
- Cut 4 (4-inch) small pocket front L squares.
- Make It Fancy! Option:
    Cut 2 (6 x 18-inch) small pocket front L rectangles.

From foam stabilizer:
- Cut 2 (18½ x 33-inch) stabilizer A rectangles.

From heavy-weight fusible interfacing:
- Cut 2 (18½ x 33-inch) interfacing A rectangles.

From fusible fleece:
- Cut 4 (4-inch) fusible fleece E small pocket squares.
- Cut 2 (8½ x 14½-inch) fusible fleece H large pocket rectangles.
- Cut 4 (10 x 4½-inch) fusible fleece I medium pocket rectangles.

Make It Fancy! Option Additional Cutting:

From fusible grid:
- Cut 2 (6½ x 8½-inch) fusible grid J rectangles.
- Cut 4 (2½ x 4-inch) fusible grid K rectangles.
- Cut 4 (4-inch) fusible grid L squares.

Make It Simple!
Use a ¼-inch seam allowance and 90/14 needle and stitch right sides together unless otherwise indicated. Refer to Basic Sewing Techniques for trimming, echo stitching, backstitching, bar tacks and topstitching.

1. Seal ends of both 4-yard pieces of webbing and set aside.

2. Fold and press B strap rectangle in half lengthwise. Open flat, fold and press both long raw edges to middle crease. Refold and press in half lengthwise again. Topstitch ¼ inch from each edge and down center of the strap. Cut strap into eight 3-inch lengths.

3. Wrap a 3-inch strap around the flat edge of a D-ring, matching raw edges. Topstitch several times across the strap as close to the D-ring as possible to secure (Figure 1).

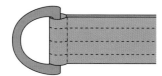

Figure 1

4. Repeat step 3 to make eight D-ring straps. Set aside.

If you wish to embellish the pockets with pleating, follow the Make It Fancy! instructions on page 41 at this point.

5. Stitch large pocket border C to the top and bottom of large pocket center J (Figure 2). Press seams away from center.

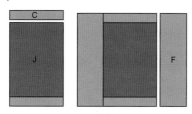

Figure 2

6. Stitch large pocket accordion F to each side of the large pocket center J referring again to Figure 2. Press seams away from center.

7. Follow manufacturer's instructions to fuse interfacing H to wrong side of the large pocket unit.

8. Topstitch on the right side of linen around the center J panel.

9. Layer and pin large pocket backing H to large pocket, leaving a 4-inch turning opening along one long edge. *Note: This is the top of the pocket.* Stitch, reinforcing corners with echo stitching; trim corners.

10. Turn right side out, using point turner to push out corners. Insert opening seam allowances to inside and press edges flat. Topstitch close to edge along the entire length of pocket top.

11. Repeat steps 5–10 for remaining large pocket and to make four medium pockets, using pieces D, G, I and K. Repeat steps 7, 9 and 10 for small pockets, using pieces E and L to complete four small pockets.

12. Accordion-fold the side of one large pocket at the top into 1-inch folds (Figure 3). Bar-tack ¼ inch below the pocket top edge, through the first and second layers of the accordion fold. Repeat on the opposite side of large pocket.

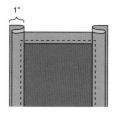

Figure 3

13. Repeat step 12 on the remaining large pocket and all four medium pockets. Set pockets aside.

14. Follow manufacturer's instructions to spray-baste stabilizer A pieces to wrong side of two exterior A pieces.

15. Follow manufacturer's instructions to fuse interfacing A pieces to the wrong side of remaining two exterior pieces.

16. Position the hanger template included on pattern insert in the upper right-hand corner of an exterior A rectangle referring to Figure 4. Trace the angled edge. Flip or rotate the template to mark each corner of all exterior pieces.

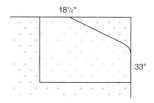

Figure 4

17. Trim corners on marked lines. Set aside the two exterior pieces with heavy-weight fusible interfacing.

18. On the right side of a foam stabilized exterior piece, mark a horizontal line 4½ inches from the top edge of the piece across the width (Figure 5). Mark a parallel line 15 inches from the top edge of the piece across the width referring again to Figure 5.

19. Mark vertical lines between the horizontal lines at 1, 2, 10, 11 and 12 inches from the exterior piece left edge and 1 inch from the exterior piece right edge referring again to Figure 5.

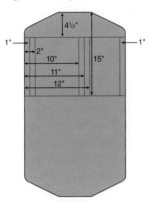

Figure 5

20. Repeat steps 18 and 19 on second foam stabilized exterior piece.

21. Baste a D-ring strap to the right side of the unmarked exterior piece ½ inch from the top corner angle referring to Figure 6. Baste remaining D-ring straps to top and bottom corners of both unmarked exterior pieces.

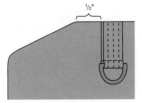

Figure 6

22. Change machine needle to size 110/18 and lengthen your stitch. Choose one marked foam stabilized exterior, one large pocket, and two each of the medium and small pockets.

23. With accordion folds pulled apart, align and pin the right and left edges of a medium pocket to the right-hand-side 1-inch vertical line and left-hand-side 12-inch vertical line. Align the pocket bottom edge on the 15-inch horizontal line marked on the exterior piece (Figure 7).

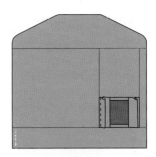

Figure 7

24. Topstitch left and right sides of pocket to exterior, backstitching at top and bottom of seam. Refold the accordion sides, evenly distributing the folds.

25. To reduce bulk at the bottom of the pocket, push the bottom of the pocket down to just below the end of the pocket and pin the top layer only (Figure 8). *Note: The accordion folds are inside the pocket, but you do not stitch through them. This makes the top of the pocket pop out at an angle.* Topstitch the bottom of the pocket through the top layer only; backstitch at each end.

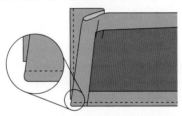

Figure 8

26. Repeat steps 23–25 for the remaining medium pocket, aligning the pocket top edge with the 4½-inch horizontal line and the sides with the right-hand-side 1-inch and left-hand-side 12-inch vertical lines Figure 9.

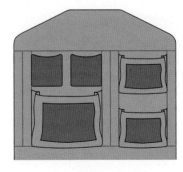

Figure 9

27. Align and pin the sides of a small pocket to the vertical 2-inch line on left-hand side and 4½-inch horizontal line. Stitch around three sides of pocket, backstitching at pocket top edges. Repeat for second small pocket, aligning the right-hand edge with the 10-inch vertical line referring again to Figure 9.

28. Repeat steps 23–25, aligning the large pocket left edge with the right-hand-side 1-inch vertical line, the right edge with the 11-inch vertical line, and the bottom edge with the 15-inch horizontal line as shown in Figure 9.

29. Repeat steps 22–28 for remaining foam stabilized exterior piece to complete two pocket units.

30. Pin pockets flat. Pin interfaced exterior pieces to pocket units leaving a 15–20-inch turning opening on one long side. Using ½-inch seam allowance and 110/18 needle, stitch around the saddlebag. Echostitch at curves and over D-ring straps.

31. Trim seams, except opening, turn right side out, pulling D-ring straps away from saddlebag, and press flat. Turn opening seam allowances to inside and topstitch outside edge of saddlebag.

TIP

The counterweight of the saddlebags and/or the weight of the mattress will lock the webbing in the D-rings. For extra security, you can tie a knot with the webbing just above the D-rings. Lay the extra webbing across the mattress. Leaving the webbing long will allow you to re-use the saddlebags on a larger or smaller bed.

32. Repeat steps 30 and 31 to make a second saddlebag.

33. Fold each saddlebag in half, with the pockets facing out and matching D-rings. On one saddlebag, take one end of one 4-yard length of webbing and lace through both D-rings. Fold the webbing back on itself and lace it back through the upper D-ring only (Figure 10). Repeat with other length of webbing and remaining D-rings.

Figure 10

34. Repeat step 33, making sure the webbing is not twisted, with the second saddlebag.

35. Install the saddlebags either between the mattress and box spring, or underneath the mattress cover. ∎

I have always done pleats the hard way—marking the folds, pressing up each one, folding it back on itself, etc. For that reason I've never attempted a pleat any smaller than 1 inch apart. I had no idea there was a thing such as a Perfect Pleater. If you don't have one, you should get one just for the pure joy of embellishing this project!

Use the Make It Fancy! option materials and cutting instructions.

1. Loosen up the louvers of the pleater by rolling it between your hands with the louvers facing out. Starting with large pocket center J, pin the 9-inch end of J right side up to ironing surface using glass-head pins.

2. With the louvers opening away from you, position the Perfect Pleater underneath the fabric.

3. Follow the manufacturer's instructions for pleating the fabric and setting your pleats. To watch an instructional video about the Perfect Pleater, go to: http://www.youtube.com/watch?v=487FDptYB88&feature=player_detailpage. *Note: I used a piece of muslin and a spray bottle of water/vinegar mixture to set my pleats in 100 percent cotton fabrics.* Allow pleats to cool completely before removing them from the pleater.

4. Carefully turn pleated piece wrong side up. Adjust pleats so the piece is nice and flat.

5. Fuse fusible grid J to the wrong side of the pleated fabric following manufacturer's instructions. Trim the pleated section around the interfacing to a 6½ x 8½-inch rectangle.

6. Repeat steps 2–5 for the remaining large pocket, the medium pocket centers K with fusible grid K, and small pocket front L with fusible grid L.

Note: Each pleated medium pocket center and small pocket front makes two pockets, so position the fusible grid on the pleats so that you get two pocket fronts and trim pleated sections.

Once the pleats are secured to the interfacing, you can manipulate the pleats however you like. To keep the pleats flat, baste near the outside edges of the pleats to hold them in place.

If you want to twist the pleats, baste one edge of the pleats flat. On the opposite side, pin pleats in the opposite direction. Baste this edge to secure pleats.

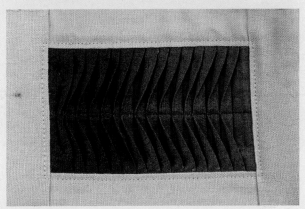

On the large pocket in this project, I stitched both edges and the center of the pleated section in the same direction, opposite to how the pleats were pressed. Have fun experimenting!

To complete this project, continue at step 5 of the Make It Simple! instructions on page 38.

These fun little buckets hang easily from a hanger, towel rack or tension rod. All sorts of things can get organized and stored this way: safety pins, tape measures, bits of ribbon, spools of thread. You can bet I'll be making some of these for my own craft room!

Hanging Buckets

Finished Size
6 inches tall (excluding handles)

Materials
Note: *Materials are given for two buckets.*

- 44/45-inch-wide woven fabrics:
  - ½ yard cotton print
  - ½ yard cotton solid
- ½ yard 44/45-inch-wide fusible fleece
- 7 x 9-inch rectangle heavy-weight fusible interfacing
- 20 inches ⅜-inch-wide ribbon
- 2 (½-inch) snaps
- Make It Fancy! Option:
  - 2 (20 x 12-inch) rectangles fusible gridded interfacing
  - 2 (20 x 12-inch) rectangles texturizing fabric product
- Basic sewing supplies and equipment

Cutting
Refer to Cutting Layouts provided on pattern insert for specific cutting instructions. Trim away selvages on fabric before cutting pieces.

From cotton print:
- Cut 2 (15 x 9-inch) exterior A rectangles.
  Make It Fancy! Option:
- Cut 2 (20 x 12-inch) exterior A rectangles.

From cotton solid:
- Cut 2 (15 x 9½-inch) lining B rectangles.
- Cut 1 (7 x 9-inch) C strap rectangle.

From fusible fleece:
- Cut 2 (15 x 9-inch) interfacing A rectangles.
  Make It Fancy! Option:
- Cut 2 (20 x 12-inch) interfacing A rectangles.

Make It Simple!
Use a ½-inch seam allowance and 80/12 needle and stitch right sides together unless otherwise indicated. Refer to Basic Sewing Techniques for trimming seam allowances, backstitching and topstitching. **Note:** *When using the Make It Fancy!*

instructions and texturizing the baskets, begin construction with 20 x 12-inch exterior and fusible fleece rectangles as instructed to cut in Cutting section. Do not texturize fabric if you are using 15 x 9-inch rectangles.

1. Follow manufacturer's instructions to fuse heavy-weight interfacing to C strap rectangle.

2. Cut four 7 x 2-inch rectangles from interfaced strap rectangle. Position and trace the 2-inch circle trimming template included on the pattern insert on one end of each strap referring to Figure 1. Trim on traced line to round end.

Figure 1

3. Referring to the tip on page 8, layer two straps right sides together and stitch around the strap sides and rounded end using a ¼-inch seam allowance; reinforce seam with echo stitching. Trim and clip rounded end.

4. Turn strap right side out. Use a point turner to gently push out the curved end; press flat. Topstitch around sides and rounded edges of the strap.

5. Mark snap position ½ inch from rounded end of strap (Figure 2). Do not attach snap at this time. Set aside.

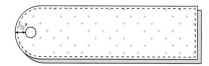

Figure 2

6. Repeat steps 3–6 to make two straps.

7. Follow manufacturer's instructions to apply fusible fleece to wrong side of exterior rectangles.

If you are embellishing the exterior fabric using texturizing fabric product, follow the Make It Fancy! instructions on page 45 at this point.

ORGANIZING TIP

Keep your fabric neat and organized by folding similar length fabrics the same way. For example, a yard of fabric or more can be wrapped around a 6-inch-wide ruler and then folded in half and stacked. Pieces that are less than a yard can be wrapped around a 4-inch-wide ruler.

8. Change machine needle to size 90/14. Fold an exterior rectangle in half right sides together matching 9-inch sides to form a tube; stitch.

9. Center seam on tube and press seam open. Stitch along bottom edge of tube with seam centered.

10. To box the exterior basket bottom, press bottom seam open. Fold basket bottom out forming a square. Refer to Figure 3 to mark and stitch 1½ inches from the corner point; trim seam to ¼ inch. Repeat on opposite corner. Turn bucket right side out.

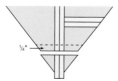

¼"

Figure 3

11. At seam on exterior bucket center back, mark 1½ inches from top edge for snap (Figure 4). Clip a few threads in the seam to inset snap; bar-tack above and below the clipped threads to reinforce seam at opening.

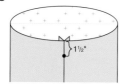

1½"

Figure 4

12. Follow manufacturer's instructions to apply male portion of snap in seam opening created at bucket center back in step 11.

13. Center and baste a strap over the back center seam, matching raw edges of top edge of bucket exterior (Figure 5). Set aside.

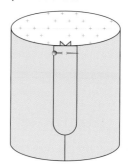

Figure 5

14. Repeat steps 8–10 with lining piece to create basket lining except leave a 3½-inch turning opening in center of back seam. Do not turn right side out.

15. Insert bucket exterior into lining right sides together, matching center back seams and top edges. Pin and stitch around top edge.

16. Turn bucket right side out through lining opening. Stitch lining opening closed by hand or machine.

17. Push lining into bucket exterior and pin the lining around the top of the bucket extending ½ inch above the bucket top. Pull up the strap and pin to the upper edge.

18. Topstitch around the upper edge of the exposed lining referring to Figure 6, stitching through the strap to secure. Stitch-in-the-ditch on the exterior and lining seam referring again to Figure 6.

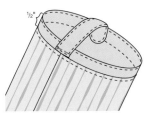

Figure 6

19. Follow manufacturer's instructions to apply the female portion of the snap to the position marked on the strap paying attention that it is facing the correct direction to form the handle.

20. Snap bucket strap over a bar or hanger to display. ■

MAKE IT FANCY! EMBELLISHING

Texturizing fabric shrinks in a predictable way (usually 30 percent), making it easy to plan enough fabric for shrinkage. You can stitch all sorts of designs in layered fashion fabric and texturizing fabric. Steam makes the texturizing fabric shrink around the stitches, creating a lovely texture in the fashion fabric. It is important to store texturizing fabric away from heat or steam before use.

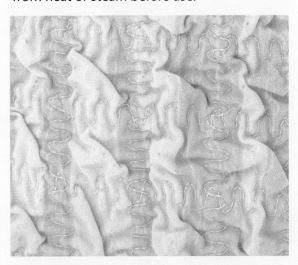

1. Fuse a gridded interfacing rectangle to the fusible fleece side of the exterior rectangles. Allow to cool completely before going to the next step.

2. Pin the texturizing fabric on top of the grid. The grid lines will show through the texturizing fabric.

3. Stitch along the lines of the grid with a straight or decorative machine stitch. A curvy stitch was used in the sample.

4. Follow the manufacturer's instructions to shrink the texturizing fabric with steam until it stops shrinking. Do not allow iron to touch the texturizing fabric.

5. Trim texturized fabric to match lining dimensions of 15 x 9½ inches.

To complete this project, continue at step 8 of the Make It Simple! instructions on page 44.

All right, I confess: I have a bad habit of not putting things back where they belong. I have sewing supplies in the living room when I'm hand-sewing, and shoes pile up by the door instead of making it up to the bedroom closet.

If you're the same way (or know someone who is), this room-to-room basket is the perfect remedy. Items that belong in a different room go in the basket, and when the basket is full, you can deliver it to the rightful owner.

Playroom Toy Baskets

Finished Size
10 x 15 x 7 inches

Materials
- 44/45-inch-wide woven fabric:
    ½ yard corduroy
    ¾ yard cotton print
    ¼ yard cotton stripe
- ½ yard 58-inch-wide foam stabilizer
- 1 (6¾ x 4½-inch) piece of clear vinyl
- 4 (⅞ x 26½-inch) strips heavy-weight fusible interfacing
- Assorted buttons
- Make It Fancy! Option:
    Coordinating felt shapes
    Embroidery floss
    Embroidery needle
- Basic sewing supplies and equipment

Cutting
Refer to Cutting Layouts provided on pattern insert for specific cutting instructions. Trim away selvages on fabric before cutting pieces.

From corduroy:
- Cut 1 (11 x 16-inch) basket bottom A rectangle.
- Cut 2 (8 x 16-inch) basket side B rectangles.
- Cut 2 (8 x 11-inch) basket end C rectangles.

From cotton print:
- Cut 1 (11 x 16-inch) lining bottom A rectangle.
- Cut 2 (8 x 16-inch) lining side B rectangles.
- Cut 2 (8 x 11-inch) lining end C rectangles.
- Cut 1 (1½ x 16-inch) pocket trim D strip.
- Cut 2 (4 x 28-inch) handle E rectangles.

From cotton stripe:
- Cut 2 (4 x 42-inch) binding F strips.

From foam stabilizer:
- Cut 1 (11 x 16-inch) foam stabilizer A rectangle.
- Cut 2 (8 x 16-inch) foam stabilizer B rectangles.
- Cut 2 (8 x 11-inch) foam stabilizer C rectangles.

Make It Simple!
Use a ½-inch seam allowance and 80/12 needle and stitch right sides together unless otherwise indicated. Refer to Basic Sewing Techniques for trimming seam allowances, backstitching, topstitching and bar tacks.

1. Stitch the binding strips together on short ends using a straight seam. Turn ¼ inch to wrong side on one short end. Press binding in half lengthwise; set aside.

2. Fold and press pocket trim strip in half lengthwise. Unfold and press long raw edges to center. Refold and press along center (Figure 1).

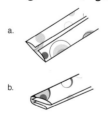

Figure 1

3. Insert long edge of vinyl piece between folds of pocket trim. Clip to hold. Topstitch trim to vinyl close to folded edges (Figure 2). Repeat on vinyl bottom, referring again to Figure 2, to complete vinyl pocket.

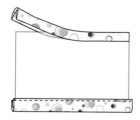

Figure 2

ORGANIZING TIP

*This basket doesn't have to be just for a
particular room—make one for every
room! Coordinate the fabric with the
room in which it belongs, and it will be
easy to tell where it goes. Don't forget to
empty the basket and put it back!*

4. Center and fuse heavy-weight fusible interfacing strips to wrong side of outside long edges of a handle following manufacturer's instructions and referring to Figure 3.

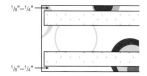

Figure 3

5. Fold and press handle referring to step 2 and Figure 1.

6. Measure and mark a line 6½ inches from each short end of handle. Topstitch ¼ inch from long edges between the marked lines.

7. Repeat steps 5 and 6 with remaining handle.

8. Spray-baste basket bottom A, basket side B and basket end C to the corresponding foam stabilizer A, B and C pieces.

9. Spray-baste lining bottom A to foam stabilizer side of basket bottom A. Set basket bottom aside.

10. Mark vertical handle placement lines on basket side B, 5½ inches from each side (Figure 4).

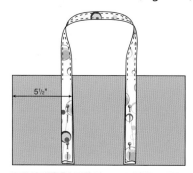

Figure 4

11. Pin handle to basket side matching unstitched ends on marked lines and raw edges to bottom, referring again to Figure 4.

12. Repeat steps 10 and 11 with remaining handle and basket side. Insert the vinyl pocket in between the open folds of handle ends on one basket side B.

13. Change machine needle to size 90/14 and topstitch handles to basket side through all layers backstitching where topstitching meets handle stitching referring to red stitching lines in Figure 5. Topstitch across the bottom edge of vinyl pocket referring again to Figure 5.

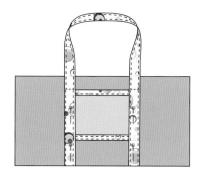

Figure 5

14. Align the lower edge of the side angle trimming template (on pattern insert) with the edge of basket side B. Mark and trim angle on both sides (Figure 6). Repeat on remaining basket side B and both basket end C pieces.

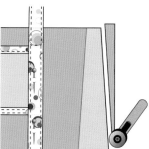

Figure 6

If you wish to embellish the sides of your basket, follow the Make It Fancy! instructions on page 50 at this point.

15. Stitch angled edges of basket side to basket end, stopping ½ inch from bottom (Figure 7).

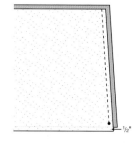

Figure 7

16. Stitch basket ends and sides together alternately as shown in Figure 8. Press seams open. Stitch the remaining open edges together to form a box; press seam open.

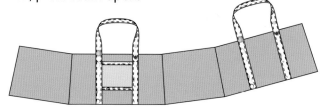

Figure 8

17. Repeat steps 14–16 with lining side and end pieces.

18. Pin handles away from top edges of basket top. Pin and stitch lining to basket right sides together around top edge matching seams.

19. Turn basket right side out and push lining to inside. Pin lining to basket along the top edge and topstitch ½ inch from top edge.

20. Match bottom edges of lining and basket, and then baste.

21. With the lining facing up, mark centers of all four sides of basket bottom. Repeat for all four sides of basket exterior.

22. Match pins and seams and pin basket exterior to basket bottom with linings facing. ***Note:*** *The ½-inch opening at the bottom of each seam will help you ease around the corner. You should see a ½-inch square of the basket bottom lining peeking out at each corner (Figure 9).*

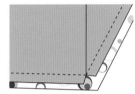

Figure 9

23. Change machine needle to size 100/16. Baste the basket sides and ends to the basket bottom, using a ½-inch seam allowance.

24. Starting with the binding folded short end, position the binding near the center back of the basket bottom. Begin stitching binding to basket 3 inches from binding end.

25. To miter corners, stop stitching ½ inch from corner with needle down. Rotate the basket 45 degrees and stitch off the corner (Figure 10a). Cut threads.

26. Fold binding up, following the angle of the corner stitching (Figure 10b). Then fold the binding back on itself down the next side (Figure 10c). ***Note:*** *You will need to adjust the position of the bulk of your basket exterior so you can continue stitching the binding.*

Figure 10

27. Repeat steps 25 and 26 to stitch all four corners. Stop stitching approximately 3 inches away from the starting end. Overlap ends of binding 1 inch and cut off excess binding. Tuck end of binding inside folded edge and pin.

28. Complete stitching of binding to basket. Fold binding to the basket bottom and stitch in place by hand.

29. To give the box more structure, use embroidery thread to bar-tack corners together by hand. Position buttons on either side of corner and stitch through corner and both buttons. ■

MAKE IT FANCY! EMBELLISHING

Hand appliqué is something I don't get to do very often, but it can be very enjoyable and relaxing. The hand embroidery stitches used to apply the appliqué need not be overly complex; if you use felted wool or bamboo and simple shapes, you can use a running stitch or simple whipstitch to secure pieces to the exterior. No fancy stitches are needed, unless you want to. Use the pattern in your cotton print for inspiration.

1. On the basket sides, mark lines 1 inch from each raw edge. Keep your embellishments inside the marked lines and they won't interfere with the basket assembly.

2. When using embroidery floss, work with 18–20-inch lengths. Stitch with two strands of embroidery thread.

3. Use a combination of felt shapes, buttons and running stitches to embellish the exterior of your basket.

To complete this project, continue at step 15 of the Make It Simple! instructions on page 48.

I don't know about you, but my desk is always littered with paper and writing implements, and I can never find my sticky notes when I need one. No more! Get things off the desk and at eye level, and have a designated spot for the things you need with this great wall organizer.

Office Wall Organizer

Finished Size
18 x 24 inches

Materials
- 1⅛ yards 44/45-inch-wide cotton stripe
- 1 yard 54-inch-wide 12–14 oz. denim
- ¼ yard 18-inch-wide clear vinyl
- ½ yard 44/45-inch-wide heavy-weight fusible interfacing
- 18 x 24-inch piece foam stabilizer
- ⁷⁄₁₆-inch metal grommet kit with hammer
- .005mm monofilament thread
- Fabric-glue stick
- Make It Fancy! Option:
    #8 pearl cotton
    embroidery needle
- Basic sewing supplies and equipment

Cutting
Refer to Cutting Layouts provided on pattern insert for specific cutting instructions. Trim away selvages on fabric before cutting pieces.

From cotton stripe:
- Cut across the width:
    5 (3-inch) pocket trim A strips.
    4 (3½-inch) binding B strips.
- Cut 1 (9 x 18-inch) grommet panel C rectangle.

From denim:
Note: *Denim has a directional nap. Follow the cutting instructions so your pockets will face the same direction.*

- Cut 2 (18 x 24-inch) exterior D rectangles.
- Cut 1 (10 x 9-inch) pocket E rectangle.
- Cut 1 (8 x 11-inch) pocket F rectangle.
- Cut 1 (7 x 18-inch) pocket G rectangle.
- Cut 1 (3 x 18-inch) pocket H rectangle.

From clear vinyl:
- Cut 1 (8-inch) pocket I square.
- Cut 1 (5½ x 4-inch) pocket J rectangle.

From heavy-weight fusible interfacing:
- Cut 1 (10 x 9-inch) interfacing E rectangle.
- Cut 1 (8 x 11-inch) interfacing F rectangle.
- Cut 1 (7 x 18-inch) interfacing G rectangle.
- Cut 1 (3 x 18-inch) interfacing H rectangle.
- Cut 1 (8 x 17-inch) interfacing K rectangle.
- Cut 1 (3½ x 17-inch) interfacing L rectangle.

Make It Simple!
Use a ½-inch seam allowance and 90/14 needle and stitch right sides together unless otherwise indicated. Refer to Basic Sewing Techniques for trimming seam allowances, backstitching, topstitching and bar tacks.

1. Fold and press a pocket trim strip in half lengthwise. Unfold the strip and press long raw edges to the center. Refold along center fold and press trim flat. Repeat for all pocket trim strips. Set aside.

2. Use a ¼-inch seam allowance and 80/12 machine needle to stitch binding strips together on short ends in one continuous strip; press seams open. Press in half lengthwise. Set aside.

3. Center and fuse interfacing K to wrong side of grommet panel C following manufacturer's instructions.

4. Press ½ inch to wrong side on long edges. Use glue stick and hot iron to hold in place.

5. Fold grommet panel in half right sides together, matching folded edges. Stitch side seams, backstitching at each end. Trim corners.

6. Fuse interfacing L to one side of grommet panel close to top fold to reinforce grommet holes (Figure 1).

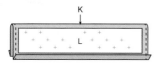

Figure 1

7. Turn grommet panel right side out; press. Referring to Figure 2, mark a horizontal line 1 inch from top fold on back of grommet panel and vertical lines 1½ inches from each side seam and 8½ inches from right-hand-side seam.

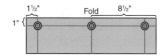

Figure 2

8. Center a grommet over the intersections of the marked lines and trace the inside of the grommet with a fabric marker. Follow the manufacturer's instructions to complete installation of all three grommets. Set aside completed grommet panel.

9. Fuse interfacing E, F, G and H to the wrong side of corresponding pockets.

10. Insert and pin pockets E, F, G, I and J top edges between folds of pocket trim strips. Insert and pin top and bottom edges of pocket H between folds of pocket trim strips. *Note: For the most efficient use of trim, use one strip for pockets F and G, one for H, and one for E, I and J.*

11. Cut the remaining trim strips into 13½- and 10½-inch lengths and set aside.

12. Topstitch pocket trim to pockets close to bottom edge of trim and along the upper fold. Trim strips even with raw edges of pockets.

13. Referring to Figure 3, mark stitching lines 3½ inches from left edge of pocket F; 2, 3½ and 5½ inches from left edge of pocket G; 6, 10 and 13½ inches from left edge of pocket H.

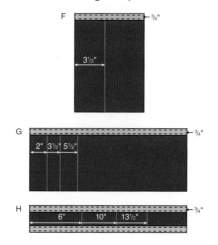

Figure 3

14. Use the edge of your point turner to crease a line 2 inches from bottom edge of pocket I.

If you wish to embellish the pockets with hand embroidery, follow the Make It Fancy! instructions on page 55 at this point.

15. Spray-baste exterior D pieces to the front and back of the foam stabilizer.

16. Mark pocket alignment lines on front of D panel across the width at 9½ and 10½ inches from bottom edge.

17. Change machine needle to size 100/16 needle and change top thread to monofilament thread.

18. Align and baste pocket F to right-hand edges of denim panel with bottom of pocket aligned with upper marked line (Figure 4).

19. Stitch along marked line on pocket F to divide pocket, backstitching at top edge, referring again to Figure 4.

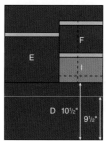

Figure 4

20. Position vinyl pocket I over pocket F, aligning bottom edges. Baste pocket I sides to D panel. Stitch pocket I along scored line 2 inches from bottom edge.

21. Align and baste pocket E to left edge of D panel and bottom of pocket along upper marked line referring again to Figure 4.

22. Center 13½-inch length of pocket trim over pocket E and F edges at center of denim panel (Figure 5). Topstitch both sides of trim, close to edge, encasing the raw edges of pockets.

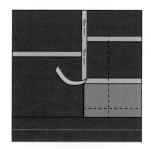

Figure 5

23. Align and baste pocket G to bottom edge of D panel referring to Figure 6. Stitch on the three marked stitching lines on pocket G, backstitching at the top edge.

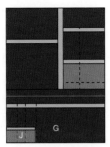

Figure 6

24. Position and baste vinyl pocket J to the lower left corner of the denim panel over pocket G referring again to Figure 6.

25. Center the 10½-inch length of pocket trim over the pocket G and J right edges starting at the lower marked horizontal line on the D panel. Topstitch both sides of pocket trim close to edges encasing the raw edges of the pockets.

26. Align lower edge of pocket H on D panel at lower chalk line, enclosing remaining raw edges of upper pockets (Figure 7). Stitch pocket H to panel along sides and lower edge. Stitch on marked lines on pocket H, backstitching at top edges.

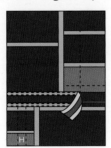

Figure 7

27. Stitch binding to front of D panel, mitering corners. Connect the ends of binding with a straight seam. Turn binding to the D panel back and handstitch in place covering seam.

28. Mark a horizontal line 2 inches from top edge of the back of the D panel. Align folded bottom edge of grommet panel on marked line and stitch to denim close to folded edge.

29. Turn the denim panel right side up and stitch in the binding seam to secure the grommet panel (Figure 8).

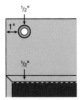

Figure 8

30. Hang wall organizer from grommets using picture hangers or hooks. ∎

MAKE IT FANCY! EMBELLISHING

Hand embroidery lends a nice touch to this wall organizer. You can label the pockets however you wish.

1. Using a disappearing fabric marker, write the words you wish to embroider on the front of each pocket. ***Note:*** *If you want to be exact, draw alignment lines using marking chalk to help keep text straight. If you make a mistake, the chalk rubs off easily.*

2. Keep embroidery at least ¾ inch from raw edges of pockets to make sure it will not be in a seam.

3. Use pearl cotton to hand-embroider the text as desired. ***Note:*** *I used a simple running stitch for mine. Don't forget to dot your i's and cross your t's! As you stitch, it's OK if you do not stitch through the layer of interfacing if it's easier for you.*

To complete this project, refer to step 15 of the Make It Simple! instructions on page 52.

Sources

Aurifil
http://www.aurifil.com

Andover Fabrics
http://www.andove
fabrics.com

Annie's
AnniesCatalog.com

Benartex LLC
http://www.benartex.com

Bohin
http://www.bohin.fr/en/

By Annie
http://www.byannie.com/

DMC
http://www.dmc-usa.com

Emma Creation
http://www.emmacreation.com

Innovative Craft Products
http://www.innovative-crafts.com/

LoveBug Studios
http://www.lovebug
studios.com

National Nonwovens
http://www.common
wealthfelt.com

ODIF USA
http://www.odifusa.com/

Pellon
http://pellonprojects.com

Prym-Dritz Corporation
http://www.dritz.com

Robert Kaufman Fabrics
http://robertkaufman.com

United Notions
http://www.unitednotions.com

Zip It
http://zipit.etsy.com

Photo Index

7

13

16

20

24

30

37

42

46

51

Annie's ®
Cut It, Sew It, Stow It is published by Annie's, 306 East Parr Road, Berne, IN 46711. Printed in USA. Copyright © 2013, 2014 Annie's. All rights reserved. This publication may not be reproduced in part or in whole without written permission from the publisher.

RETAIL STORES: If you would like to carry this pattern book or any other Annie's publications, visit AnniesWSL.com.

Every effort has been made to ensure that the instructions in this pattern book are complete and accurate. We cannot, however, take responsibility for human error, typographical mistakes or variations in individual work. Please visit AnniesCustomerCare.com to check for pattern updates.

ISBN: 978-1-59635-753-2

3 4 5 6 7 8 9